D1128569

S
28. 49

DATE DUE

MAY 1 5 2012	
MAY 1 7 2014	
APR 0 7 2015	

BRODART, CO.   Cat. No. 23-221

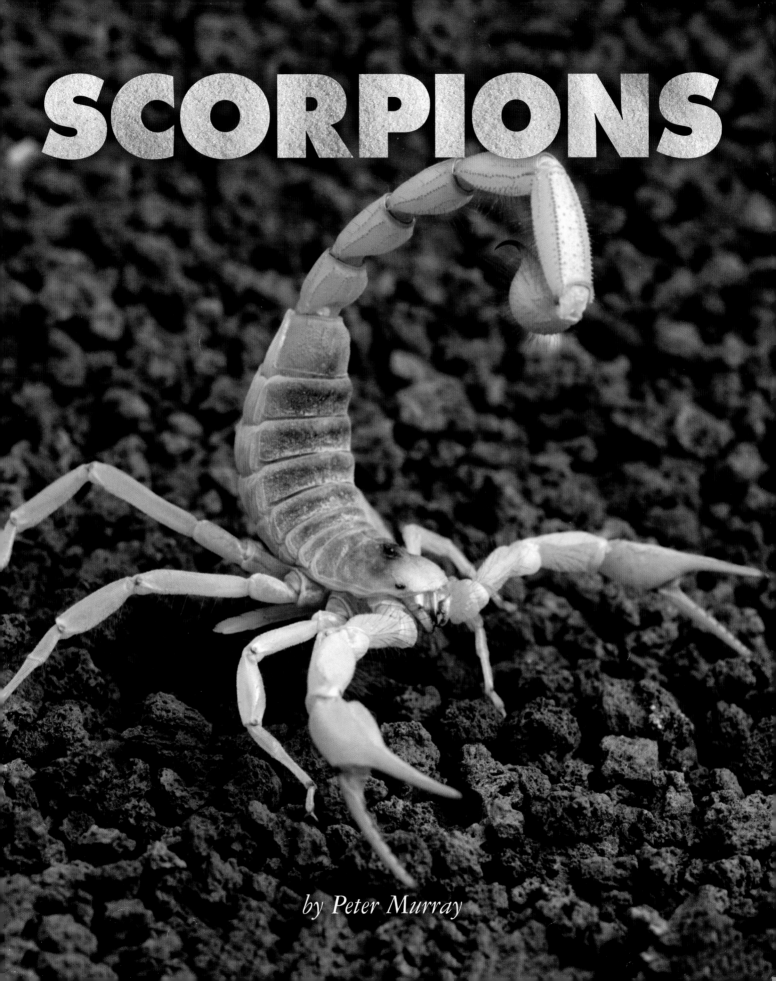

SCORPIONS

by Peter Murray

The Child's World

Published in the United States of America by The Child's World®
1980 Lookout Drive • Mankato, MN 56003-1705
800-599-READ • www.childsworld.com

PHOTO CREDITS
© Alan & Sandy Carey/zefa/Corbis: 7
© allOver photography/Alamy: 5
© David A. Northcott/Corbis: 29
© David Shale/naturepl.com: 11
© Dietmar Huber: 24
© Doug Wechsler/naturepl.com: 23
© Dr. Merlin D. Tuttle/Photo Researchers, Inc.: 27
© Fabio Colombini Medeiros/Animals Animals–Earth Scenes: 13
© iStockphoto.com/Achim Prill: 3, 31
© iStockphoto.com/Nico Smit: 19
© Joe McDonald/Animals Animals–Earth Scenes: 8–9
© John Cancalosi/Alamy: 20
© John Gerlach/Animals Animals–Earth Scenes: 24–25
© Michael & Patricia Fogden/Minden Pictures: 16–17
© Piotr Naskrecki/Minden Pictures: 15
© William Dow/Corbis: cover, 1

ACKNOWLEDGMENTS
The Child's World®: Mary Berendes, Publishing Director;
Katherine Stevenson, Editor; Pamela Mitsakos, Photo Researcher;
Judy Karren, Fact Checker

The Design Lab: Kathleen Petelinsek, Design and Page Production

LIBRARY OF CONGRESS CATALOGING-IN-PUBLICATION DATA
Murray, Peter, 1952 Sept. 29–
  Scorpions / by Peter Murray.
    p. cm. — (New naturebooks)
  Includes index.
  ISBN-13: 978-1-59296-852-7 (library bound : alk. paper)
  ISBN-10: 1-59296-852-X (library bound : alk. paper)
 1. Scorpions—Juvenile literature. I. Title.
  QL458.7.M88 2007
  595.4'6—dc22   2006103457

Copyright © 2008 by The Child's World®
All rights reserved. No part of this book may be reproduced or utilized in
any form or by any means without written permission from the publisher.

Table of Contents

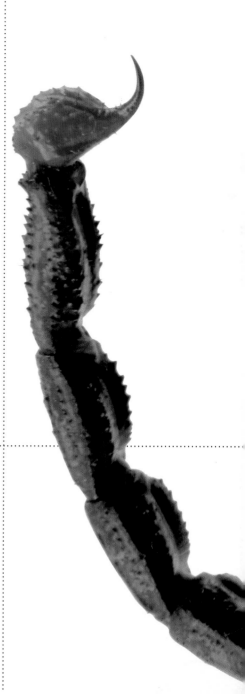

On the cover: Desert hairy scorpions like this one live in the southwestern United States.

Meet the Scorpion!

Scorpions look a little like lobsters, but they're actually related to spiders.

All over the world, scorpions have been a part of people's stories for thousands of years.

When night comes, the desert seems very still. But under the ground, and beneath the rocks, and in the hollows of dead trees, things are moving. A beetle crawls out from under a rock. Nearby, a strange-looking animal waits, motionless. The animal has eight legs, crab-like claws, and a tail that curves over its back. The beetle crawls closer. Finally the odd-looking animal pounces—and the beetle becomes dinner. What is this nighttime hunter? It's a scorpion!

Common yellow scorpions like this one can be found in many places. This one was crawling on some rocks in Portugal.

What Are Scorpions?

Ticks and mites are arachnids, too.

The oldest known arachnid fossils are scorpions. Some scorpion fossils are well over 400 million years old.

When scorpions run, they hold their pincers outstretched.

Scorpions, along with spiders, belong to a group of animals called **arachnids**. Arachnids have eight legs and a body with two main parts—a *cephalothorax* (SEH-fuh-luh-THOR-ax) and an *abdomen*. Arachnids' bodies are covered with a hard, waterproof shell called an **exoskeleton**.

Scorpions have long, slender bodies with curved tails that end in a stinger. The stinger can shoot poisonous **venom** into a victim. Besides their eight legs, scorpions have a pair of *pedipalps* with crab-like pincers. Scorpions use both their pincers and their stingers to hunt and to protect themselves.

Asian forest scorpions like this one can grow to be 5 inches (13 cm) long. These scorpions live in Malaysia and Indonesia.

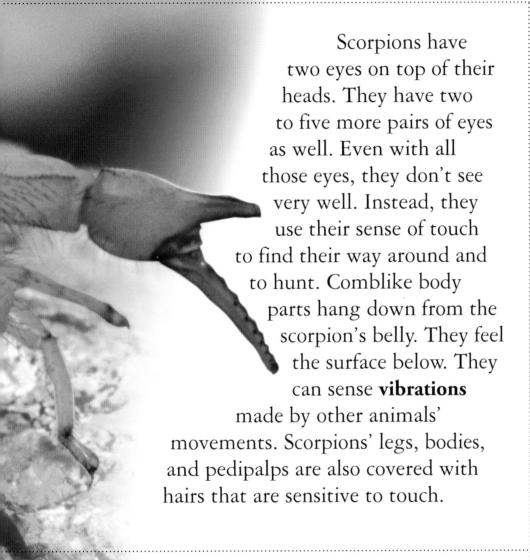

Scorpions have two eyes on top of their heads. They have two to five more pairs of eyes as well. Even with all those eyes, they don't see very well. Instead, they use their sense of touch to find their way around and to hunt. Comblike body parts hang down from the scorpion's belly. They feel the surface below. They can sense **vibrations** made by other animals' movements. Scorpions' legs, bodies, and pedipalps are also covered with hairs that are sensitive to touch.

You can clearly see the body parts of this desert hairy scorpion.

Scorpions' bodies are flat. That lets the animals squeeze into cracks or hide under rocks or bark.

A scorpion's exoskeleton has a waxy coating that keeps the animal from drying out.

Are There Different Kinds of Scorpions?

Some scorpions hold their stingers up over their backs. Others usually carry their stingers off to one side.

There are perhaps 1,500 different kinds, or **species**, of scorpions in the world. The smallest are only one-half inch (a little over a centimeter) long. The largest are African scorpions that grow to over 8 inches (20 cm)! Most kinds of scorpions are 2 to 3 inches (5 to 8 cm) long. There are about 90 kinds of scorpions that live in the United States.

Giant African scorpions are also called emperor scorpions or imperial scorpions. They live in Africa's warm, wet rain forests.

Where Do Scorpions Live?

In the U.S., scorpions are most common in Arizona, Texas, and Oklahoma.

The biggest scorpion species in the U.S. is the desert hairy scorpion. It often grows 5 inches (13 cm) long.

Most scorpions live alone. A few kinds live in groups.

Most scorpions live in warm places, especially deserts. But they can live in a wide range of places, from grasslands to rain forests. Some kinds even live in caves. Scorpions are found in North, Central, and South America as well as in Europe, Africa, and Asia. They have even been found living 12,000 feet (3,658 m) high in the Andes Mountains! In areas with cold winters, scorpions go into a deep sleep for the winter.

Most scorpions are **nocturnal** animals that hide during the day in cool, moist spots and come out at night. They like to hide under rocks or bark or other objects. Some dig burrows into the soil. Those that dig burrows usually spend most of their time inside them. When they come out, they don't go very far.

Brazilian yellow scorpions like this one are very dangerous. This one was found just outside the city of São Paulo.

What Do Scorpions Eat?

Scorpions sometimes drink water. But mostly they get all the water they need from their food.

Scorpions are **predators** that eat lots of different **prey** such as insects, spiders, and worms. They even eat other scorpions. Larger scorpions can eat larger prey animals such as small lizards, snakes, or mice. Most scorpions hunt by sitting still and waiting for their prey to come to them. Those that dig burrows often wait in or near the burrow's entrance. But some scorpions don't just wait for their dinner—they go stalking it instead.

This close-up photo shows a scorpion feeding on a cricket. You can see the scorpion's pinching mouthparts.

When scorpions feel a prey animal moving nearby, they grab it with their pincers. Sometimes they use their stinger to **paralyze** the prey, especially if the animal is large. The pincers crush the prey and pull it toward the scorpion. The scorpion's powerful jaws tear the prey open. Special juices break down the prey's insides, and the scorpion chews and sucks down its dinner. Scorpions are slow eaters. It might take the whole night for a scorpion to finish its meal. Then it will crawl back under a rock or a log and not eat again for days.

Scorpions' strong jaws chew and grind their prey with a sawing motion.

Scorpions can live for a while without eating. They might go two weeks—or even two months—between meals.

This Namib dune scorpion has also caught a cricket to eat. You can see how the scorpion uses its pincers to pull the meal toward its mouth.

17

How Dangerous Are Scorpions?

Each species of scorpion makes its own type of venom.

The most dangerous types of scorpions live in North Africa, the Middle East, India, and Mexico.

Once a scorpion uses its venom, it needs up to two weeks to make more. During that time, the scorpion can't sting.

A scorpion's venom is strong enough to kill a spider, a beetle, or a mouse. But the venom of most kinds isn't deadly to people. To a person, a scorpion sting is usually like getting stung by a bee. But some scorpions have powerful venom that can make a person very sick. There are about 25 kinds of scorpions in the world that are truly dangerous to people.

Scorpion venom is most dangerous for people who are very young, very old, or ill. Like bee stings, scorpion stings are also dangerous for people who are **allergic** to the venom.

African yellow-leg scorpions like this one live in South Africa. This one is upset and has raised its tail high—ready to strike!

Scorpion stings happen by accident. Scorpions sometimes wander into houses at night looking for something to eat. In the morning, when it gets light, they hide in small, dark places. Outdoors, they might hide in old logs or under rocks. But inside, they might hide under bedcovers or in the toe of a shoe. If people accidentally disturb a scorpion, either inside or outdoors, they can get stung.

In the U.S., the only scorpions with dangerous venom are bark scorpions and their close relatives. These yellowish scorpions grow to about 3 inches (almost 8 cm) long. They have slender pincers and a thin tail that curls to the side. They live only in certain parts of the Southwest.

Bark scorpions can squeeze through a crack only one-sixteenth of an inch (less than 2 mm) wide.

Bark scorpions can climb rocks and walls very well, so they can easily get inside. They're attracted to the moisture around people's homes. People often find them in cellars, attics, or piles of firewood.

This bark scorpion was found in Arizona. Bark scorpions are commonly found around trees, especially ones near streams.

What Are Baby Scorpions Like?

When scorpions mate, the male holds the female's pincers while the two go through a lengthy "courtship dance."

Some kinds of scorpions carry their growing babies for up to a year and a half.

Many kinds of scorpions have about 25 to 35 babies at a time.

Scorpions don't hatch from eggs. Instead, they're born as tiny scorpions. After mating, the female carries the babies for several months as they develop inside clear sacs. When most scorpion mothers give birth, they fold their legs into a "birth basket" for catching the babies. As soon as the babies are born, they crawl out of the sacs and onto their mother's back. That's where they live for their first week or two.

Here you can see a mother scorpion carrying her young on her back. How many do you see?

As a young scorpion grows, its hard exoskeleton quickly becomes too small. The scorpion must **molt**, or shed, the old exoskeleton. The exoskeleton splits, and the baby wriggles out. At first, the outside of its body is soft. Then the new exoskeleton hardens.

Scorpion babies molt for the first time when they are about one or two weeks old. Along with new, bigger exoskeletons, the young scorpions now have the ability to sting! They leave their mothers and fend for themselves. Scorpions molt five to eight times before they are fully grown.

Scorpions are most in danger after they molt, when their bodies are still soft.

This freshly shed exoskeleton still looks like a real scorpion! It was found in Arizona.

25

Do Scorpions Have Enemies?

Scorpions' bodies contain lots of fat. They make a good meal for animals that don't mind the risk of being stung.

Most scorpions in the wild live from 2 to 10 years. In zoos, some live to be 25.

Even though scorpions have stingers, lots of other animals like to eat them. Some spiders, insect-eating lizards, and centipedes all eat scorpions. So do some kinds of birds, especially owls. Other small animals such as bats, shrews, and grasshopper mice hunt scorpions, too. Even scorpions eat other scorpions!

This pallid bat has found an adult scorpion to eat.

Are Scorpions Important?

Scorpions glow brightly under special ultraviolet lights. That can make it easier to find them around someone's home.

People who live near scorpions learn to be careful. They don't go barefoot, especially at night. They shake out their shoes, clothes, and bedding. And they close off places where scorpions can get inside.

Scorpions have been around longer than people! Like all animals, they have an important place on the planet. They eat lots of termites and other insects, and they provide food for other animals. In some areas, scorpions can be a real nuisance for people. But usually they are harmless.

Perhaps a zoo or nature center near you keeps scorpions you can see. They are interesting animals to watch! And learning about them will help you see how they fit into the natural world.

28

This desert hairy scorpion does not like how close the photographer has come. It is ready to strike!

Glossary

allergic (uh-LUR-jik) When animals or people are allergic to something, their bodies do not react well to it. Some people are allergic to scorpion venom.

arachnids (uh-RAK-nidz) Arachnids are boneless animals that have eight legs, two main body parts (a cephalothorax and an abdomen), and no wings. Scorpions are arachnids.

exoskeleton (ek-soh-SKEH-luh-tun) An exoskeleton is a hard outside covering on an animal. Scorpions have an exoskeleton.

molt (MOLT) To molt is to get rid of an old outer layer of skin, shell, hair, or feathers. Scorpions molt their exoskeleton as they grow.

nocturnal (nok-TUR-nul) An animal that is nocturnal is active mostly at night and rests during the day. Most scorpions are nocturnal.

paralyze (PEH-ruh-lyze) When an animal is paralyzed, it can no longer move. A scorpion's venom paralyzes its victims.

predators (PREH-duh-terz) Predators are animals that hunt and kill other animals for food. Scorpions are predators.

prey (PRAY) Prey are animals that other animals hunt as food. Insects are often prey for scorpions.

species (SPEE-sheez) An animal species is a group of animals that share the same features and can have babies only with animals in the same group. There are perhaps 1,500 species of scorpion.

venom (VEN-um) Venom is a poisonous substance some animals produce. They can harm other animals with it, usually by biting or stinging. Scorpions produce venom.

vibrations (vy-BRAY-shunz) Vibrations are rapid, back-and-forth movements. Scorpions can sense vibrations.

To Find Out More

Read It!

Halfmann, Janet. *Scorpions*. San Diego, CA: Kidhaven Press, 2003.

Hillyard, P. D., and Steve Johnson. *A Look Inside Spiders and Scorpions*. Pleasantville, NY: Reader's Digest Young Families, 1995.

Lassieur, Allison. *Scorpions: The Sneaky Stingers*. New York: Franklin Watts, 2000.

Packard, Mary. *The Real Thing! Scorpions*. New York, Scholastic, 2005.

Pringle, Laurence, and Gary A. Polis (photographer). *Scorpion Man: Exploring the World of Scorpions*. New York: C. Scribner's Sons, 1994.

On the Web

Visit our Web page for lots of links about scorpions:
http://www.childsworld.com/links

Note to Parents, Teachers, and Librarians: We routinely check our Web links to make sure they're safe, active sites—so encourage your readers to check them out!

31

Index

About the Author

Peter Murray has written more than a hundred children's books on science, nature, history, and other topics. An animal lover, Pete lives in Golden Valley, Minnesota, in a house with one woman, two poodles, several dozen spiders, thousands of microscopic dust mites, and an occasional mouse.